RHAPSODY

RHAPSODY

Kelly Wearstler

with

Amanda Luttrell Garrigus

New York Paris London Milan

08 – 55
CURATED COMPOSITIONS

56 – 101
FETISH OF FORM

102 – 155
RAW AND REFINED

156 – 199
METALLIFEROUS

200 – 247
CHROMA CONSTRUCTION

248 – 255
INDEX AND APPLAUSE

CURATED COMPOSITIONS

A BEAUTIFUL VIGNETTE, A CAPTIVATING MISE-EN-SCÈNE, THESE GATHERINGS OF MEANINGFUL OBJECTS,

placed together in deliberate but emotional arrangements, are opportunities to showcase personal objects of desire while also heightening the complexity and therefore interest in a given space. To me these mise-en-scènes are curatorial projects in the truest sense of the word. They can be created on a large scale utilizing furniture and architecture, and equally well on a very small scale, as with crystal boxes on a marble bathroom countertop.

When I am designing a home, I give as much attention to the placement of a decorative chair as I do to the hanging of an expansive painting, in every instance engaging the interplay of texture and scale. For example, I have placed an oversized, abstract, organic metal-leafed sculpture on a large marble dining table under a brilliant, linear crystal chandelier. The juxtaposition of those two objects created a striking tableau, affecting the space with its compelling tension. On a smaller scale, in a woman's master bath, I placed petite boxes of differing sizes and materials, allowing for greater organization but also creating a visually exciting vista. A well-considered vignette can make a piece of art all the more beautiful by adding a complementary energy and form.

When your eye travels around a space, it should be captivated by every view, whether by a dominating architectural feature or a moveable tablescape. To my thinking there is no place for rigidity in design. Be willing to move objects from place to place in a room, or from room to room in a house, regardless of your initial intentions. A sculpture meant for an entryway might sit better alongside a favored painting in a study or a child's room. Use your intuition. If something feels good, then it's right.

It is true that most of my clients collect art and sculpture, and these typically figure prominently in each of their curated vignettes. But, like most of us, they also have objects, large and small, collected from their travels around the world and through their lives, touchstones and markers of important moments in their personal history. We all have these sentimental objects among our possessions, and when each is thoughtfully placed, grouped together in energetically and visually complex ways, they create the essence of what will become a warm and wonderful home.

MY INSPIRATION TRAY IS A LIBRARY OF ALL
THE ELEMENTS IN A GIVEN ROOM. EACH PIECE
IS LOOSE AND FREE-FLOATING TO ACCOMMODATE
THE INEVITABLE CHANGES THAT WILL ARISE
OVER THE COURSE OF A PROJECT.

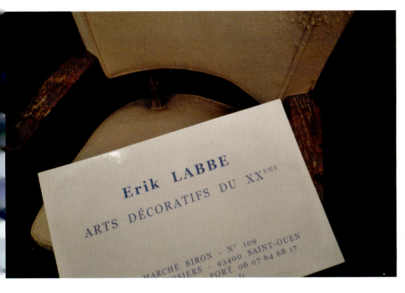

I TAKE HUNDREDS OF PHOTOS A WEEK, SO TO ORGANIZE WHAT I'VE SEEN I TAKE A PHOTOGRAPH OF THE BUSINESS CARDS OF THE SHOPS I'VE VISITED, AND THE SIGNAGE ON EACH OF THE PIECES I'M CONSIDERING. THEY ACT LIKE VISUAL INDEX CARDS.

IN SOME CASES, A PARED-DOWN VIGNETTE CAN MAKE A POWERFUL STATEMENT. THIS SINGLE, IMPORTANT CHAIR, SET AGAINST A BEAUTIFUL PINK ONYX WALL, CREATES A STRIKING IMAGE.

EVEN THE ARCHITECTURAL ELEMENTS OF A ROOM DESERVE CURATORIAL CONSIDERATION, FROM SOURCING THE PERFECT MARBLE AT THE STONE YARD TO CHOOSING THE MOST FLATTERING LIGHTING. DRAWER PULLS, DOOR KNOBS, FAUCETS, SINKS . . . EVERY ELEMENT REQUIRES THOUGHTFUL ATTENTION.

THE RUG IN THIS STUDY HAS SUCH BEAUTIFUL MOVEMENT, AND I WANTED TO CREATED THE SAME ENERGY ON THE WALL ELEVATION. I ACCOMPLISHED THIS BY COVERING ONE WALL WITH BLACK-AND-WHITE PHOTOGRAPHS, SHOWCASING THEM IN MANY DIFFERENT FRAME AND MATTE SIZES. THIS GAVE EACH IMAGE ITS OWN VOICE AND CREATED THE DIMENSION AND DEPTH NECESSARY FOR THEM TO COEXIST WITH THE STRIKING FLOOR

THE PICTURES I TAKE ARE VERTICAL OR HORIZONTAL DEPENDING ON WHAT BEST SUITS THE ITEM I'M SHOOTING. AN UPRIGHT MIRROR, FOR EXAMPLE, IS BEST REPRESENTED IN A VERTICAL PHOTOGRAPH, WHILE A LOW, WIDE DRESSER IS MOST APPROPRIATELY FRAMED HORIZONTALLY. THESE IMAGES ARE THE FIRST STEPS IN MY CURATORIAL PROCESS.

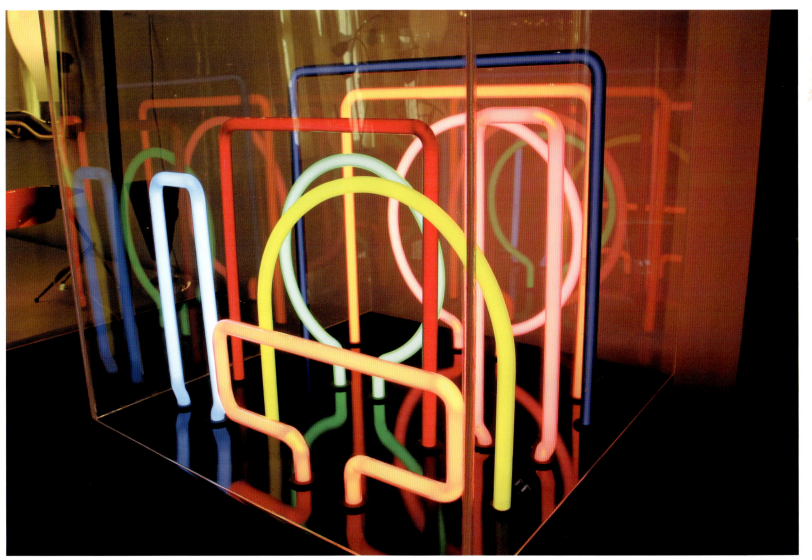

ALL OF THESE ELEMENTS PLAY OFF ONE ANOTHER: THE BOLD, CHILI-CORAL WALL COLOR, THE ORGANIC FORM OF THE BRANCHES, AND THE BEAUTIFUL GREEN APPLES, JUXTAPOSED WITH THE LINEAR GRAPHIC SCULPTURE. IF EVEN ONE OF THESE ITEMS WERE NOT THERE, THE END RESULT WOULD BE ENTIRELY DIFFERENT. TOGETHER, THEY COMPLETE ONE ANOTHER.

FETISH OF FORM

NEVER UNDERESTIMATE THE POWER

I WANTED TO CREATE SOMETHING VERY
FREE-FORM AND ALLURING IN THIS SPACE.
THE ORGANIC SWEEP OF THE STAIRCASE
JUXTAPOSED AGAINST THE GRAPHIC
FEATURES OF THE GRAND STAIR VESTIBULE
MANIFESTS A KIND OF SEXUAL TENSION.

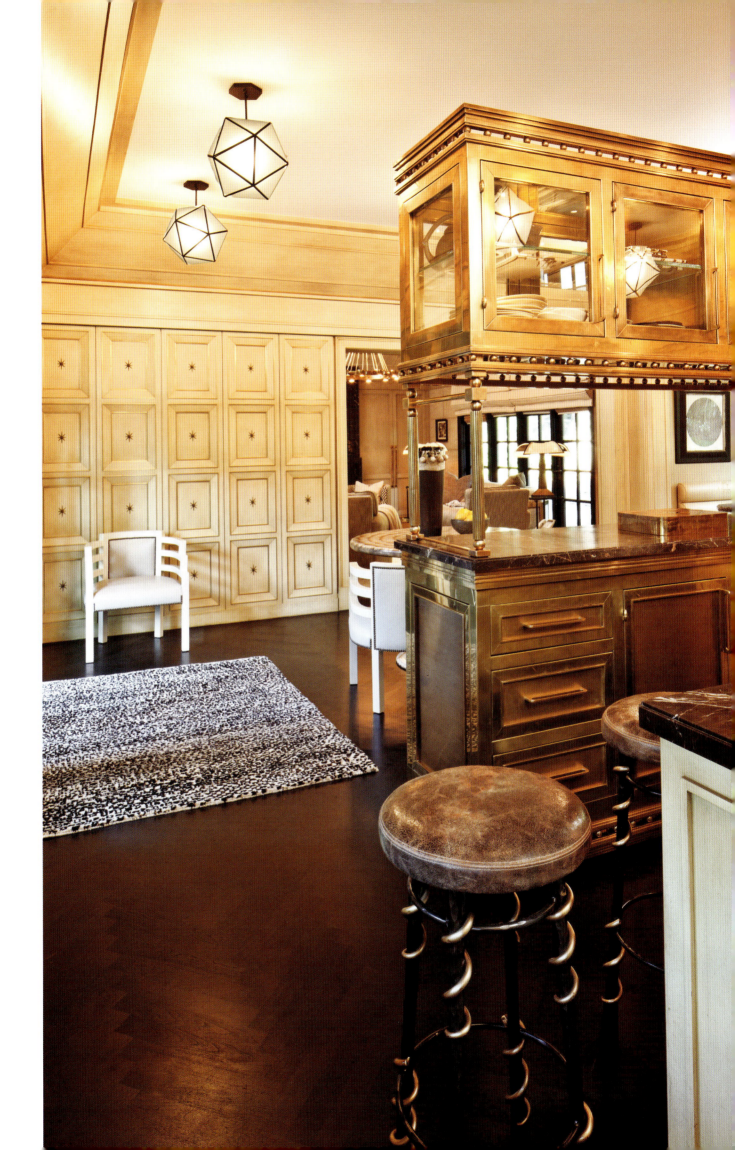

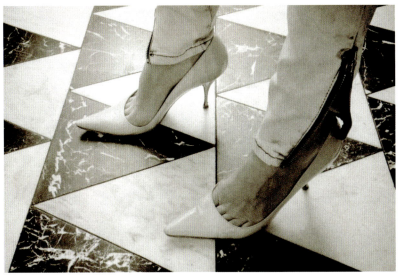
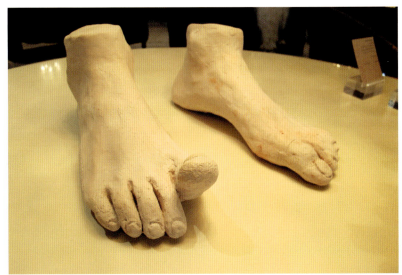

I LOOK AT EVERY PIECE AS THOUGH IT WERE SCULPTURE. EACH INDIVIDUAL ELEMENT HAS ITS OWN VOICE. WHEN I AM SHOPPING I CONSIDER THE DIALOGUE IT WILL HAVE WITH THE OTHER FEATURES OF THE PROJECT.

THIS IS AN EXCELLENT EXAMPLE OF HOW A VARIETY OF FORMS COEXIST BEAUTIFULLY. ON THE WALL HANGS A 1970S FRENCH STAINLESS-STEEL ORGANICALLY RHYTHMIC SCULPTURE. THE FLOOR SHOWCASES A CARPET WITH A RIGID GRID FORMAT, AND THE HANDRAIL STANDS ITS GROUND WITH A REPEATED ARCH PATTERN.

GOLD-LEAF PLASTER PLACED WITH A GRAPHIC
EBONY PARQUET FLOOR, WHICH MIGHT THEN SIT
ALONGSIDE A HAMMERED METAL ELEMENT . . .
EACH FABRICATED AND INSTALLED TO CREATE
UNIQUE, UNEXPECTED FORMS THAT WILL
ULTIMATELY BRING DEPTH AND INTEREST TO
A SPACE.

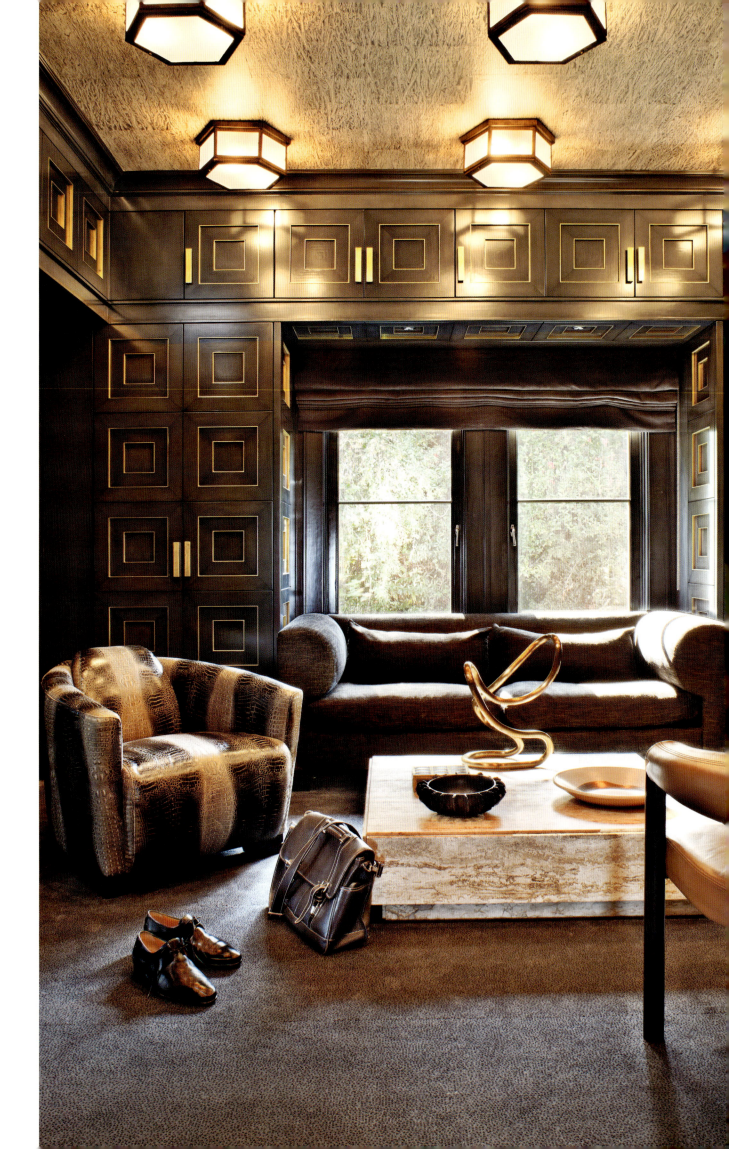

THE FREE-SPIRITED BRUSHSTROKE OF THIS HAND-PAINTED WALL COVERING SITS BEAUTIFULLY ALONGSIDE THE GRAPHIC ONE-HUNDRED-KNOT-PER-SQUARE-INCH SILK CARPET. VARYING SHAPES OF FURNITURE, SCULPTURE, AND ART COMPLEMENT ONE ANOTHER BEAUTIFULLY.

I LOOK TO MOTHER NATURE AND THE FIGURAL FORM TO BRING SOUL AND LIFE TO A ROOM, WHETHER IT'S AN ANIMAL, A BEAUTIFUL SLAB OF MARBLE, OR A BUST.

SOMETIMES MORE IS MORE . . . A STRIPE ON THE WALLS, A MARBLE GRAPHIC-PATTERNED FLOOR, AND A MODERNE ART DECO-INSPIRED ANTIQUE SILVER-LEAF CLOSET . . . ALL THESE GRAPHIC FORMS COME TOGETHER TO TELL ONE BEAUTIFUL STORY.

RAW AND REFINED

SOME OF THE MOST INTERESTING PEOPLE I HAVE EVER MET ARE THOSE WITH A RICH APPRECIATION FOR AND KNOWLEDGE OF THE PAST, AS WELL AS AN ACTIVE INTEREST IN MODERN ISSUES AND IDEAS.

You could carry on a conversation with them for hours, and never lose interest. When I consider the design of a room, I think of creating intrigue in much the same way. By introducing antiques to their contemporary counterparts, I can create a tension that engages its inhabitants in an enthralling and rich dialogue. I am fearless in my approach, and I'm always encouraging my clients to be the same. I introduce disparate elements, bringing together unlikely pairings in my attempt to achieve a look that is at once soulful and glamorous, contemporary and of a bygone era. I find that mixing raw, rough-hewn organic components with refined classic detailing in a space with pristine architectural features creates a variance that adds complexity and incites conversation.

A Jackson Pollack-inspired gray-and-white-splattered-paint wallpaper can form the backdrop for a beautiful classic sculpture, which itself offsets traditional molding and millwork in a staircase vestibule. The curious adjacency of rough-hewn tie-dyed suede upholstered onto an exquisitely beautiful art deco chair can frame a master bedroom entry; the rawness of a honed marble floor in a gentleman's master bath can sit in beautiful contrast to the refined proportion and scale of its pattern. These juxtapositions give a space tension, enchantment, and together make a luxurious interior less intimidating and infinitely more livable.

At times a client will request that every element in their home be new. In those instances I will commission pieces from a wide array of craftspeople and artisans, so each piece has a different energy, a different hand. A space that is entirely new and uniform lacks the soulfulness that can make a room feel like a brilliantly engaging old friend, rather than a cool, unapproachable acquaintance.

Rawness and refinement are not opposite ends of a luxurious spectrum; quite the contrary, they are two complementary features with which to populate a luxe environment.

THE MASCULINE QUALITY OF THIS HAND-SCULPTED CERAMIC TILE AND THE SINEWY FEMININITY OF THE BIRD SCULPTURES PROVIDE THE PERFECT EXAMPLE OF SUCCESSFULLY COMBINING RAWNESS AND REFINEMENT.

THE RAWNESS OF PATINAED-COPPER DETAILING, AND THE REFINEMENT OF A SILK VELVET FABRIC; THE ROUGH-HEWN HEMP HERRINGBONE RUG, AND THE EXQUISITELY CRAFTED ONE-HUNDRED-KNOT-PER-SQUARE-INCH REFINED SILK CARPET; UNENCUMBERED TIGER'S-EYE QUARTZITE AND FINELY CRAFTED STRAW MARQUETRY WALL PANELING . . . MATERIAL CONTRADICTIONS LIKE THESE CREATE BEAUTIFUL TENSION

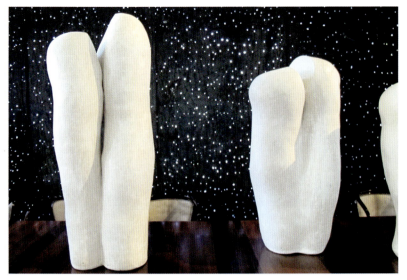 

I LIKE HAVING THE TENSION OF SOMETHING RAW AND REFINED IN A ROOM. THE TENSION CAN COME FROM TWO SEPARATE OBJECTS, OR BOTH QUALITIES MIGHT EXIST IN A SINGLE PIECE.

FROM THE VINTAGE FRENCH CHAIRS UPHOLSTERED
IN TIE-DYED SUEDE TO THE HAND-PAINTED WALL
COVERING AND THE ALABASTER LAMP AND CARA-
MEL-COLORED SNAKE CONSOLE, NEARLY EVERY
ELEMENT IN THIS ROOM ADDS ENERGETICALLY
TO THE RAWNESS OF THE COMPLETE VISION.
THE 1960S MURANO GLASS CHANDELIERS ADD
A FEMININE ELEGANCE TO THE OTHERWISE
ENTIRELY ORGANIC VIGNETTE.

WHEN I SEE THINGS, WHEN I STOP TO TAKE A PHOTO, I AM ALWAYS EXPERIENCING AN EMOTIONAL AS WELL AS A VISUAL CONNECTION. I AM DRAWN EQUALLY TO THINGS MADE BY SKILLED CRAFTSMAN, LIKE A BRONZE SCULPTURE, AND TO THINGS GIVEN BIRTH BY MOTHER NATURE, LIKE AN EXQUISITE PIECE OF MARBLE.

SOMETIMES A SINGLE ELEMENT CAN BE AT
ONCE RAW AND REFINED, AS WITH THIS
GLAMOROUS ALPACA CHAIR AND THE TWO-
STORY STAN BITTERS FIREPLACE SURROUND
BESIDE WHICH IT SITS. THE SINGULARLY
REFINED COPPER CABINET TEMPERS THESE
TWO FIERCE ELEMENTS.

OF THE MANY STRIKING FEATURES OF THIS ROOM,
THE ART ON THE WALLS PERHAPS BEST ILLUSTRATES
THE EVOCATIVE TENSION CREATED BY A COMING
TOGETHER OF RAW AND REFINED IDEOLOGIES.
THE MAN RAY PHOTOGRAPHS, THE WALL PORTRAIT,
THE UNFRAMED ARTIST CANVASES ARE EACH
FURTHER ENLIVENED BY THEIR PROXIMITY TO
THE PAUL EVANS BRUTALIST CREDENZA.

METALLIFEROUS

I HAVE HAD A LONG-STANDING LOVE AFFAIR WITH METAL. IT IS GLAMOROUS AND SEXY, RICH AND EVOCATIVE.

From the cool, stark brilliance of gold and silver plate to the complex, warm, organic qualities of a patinaed bronze, and even further to a bolt of metallic leather fabric, employing metalliferous elements is one of the most impactful ways I have found to imbue a room with depth, character, and luxury. Whether I introduce metallurgy through the more obvious, literal use of sculpture or in the bold frame of a heavy antique mirror, or by more subtle means, as with inlaid details in wooden cabinetry, the results are the same: a spirit and a luster that can be achieved in no other way so effectively.

Sometimes I will encourage a client who is resistant to the idea of mixing metals—silver with gold, for example—to reach beyond their ideas of uniformity so that they might experience something extraordinary. I will suggest to them, and then show them, that it is exactly this mixing of contrasting materials that creates a unique finish to a room, that makes it at once luxurious, thoughtful, exquisitely comfortable, and yet engagingly complex. Contrast and contradiction are what create drama and excitement.

Metal can play a starring role in a room, as with a striking bronze kitchen étagère, or it can impact an interior vista from the background, as evidenced by a hand-troweled wallpaper dripping with gold from the walls of a master bedroom suite. Silver, gold, copper, and bronze are like jewelry for interiors. Metal commingles beautifully with other materials, instantly giving its companion substance a richness and depth it may otherwise have lacked and thereby elevating it to a new level of luxe. Whether metal becomes a defining principle or plays only a supporting role, it is an important feature of every project I undertake.

I LEFT THE BEAUTIFUL BRONZE RAILING ON THIS STAIRCASE UNLACQUERED SO THAT IT WOULD ACQUIRE A PATINA, AND THEREFORE IMPROVE WITH AGE.

I WANTED METAL AS A STRIKING BACKDROP FOR THE MANUSCRIPT LIBRARY IN THIS MUSIC ROOM, SO I SKINNED THE CEILING WITH A PIGMENTED GOLD-LEAF WASH, THEN SELECTED A BEAUTIFUL 18^(TH)-CENTURY LADDER IN ANTIQUED BRASS AND SILVER WITH COPPER DETAILS AND ART LIBRARY LAMPS IN ANTIQUED BRONZE

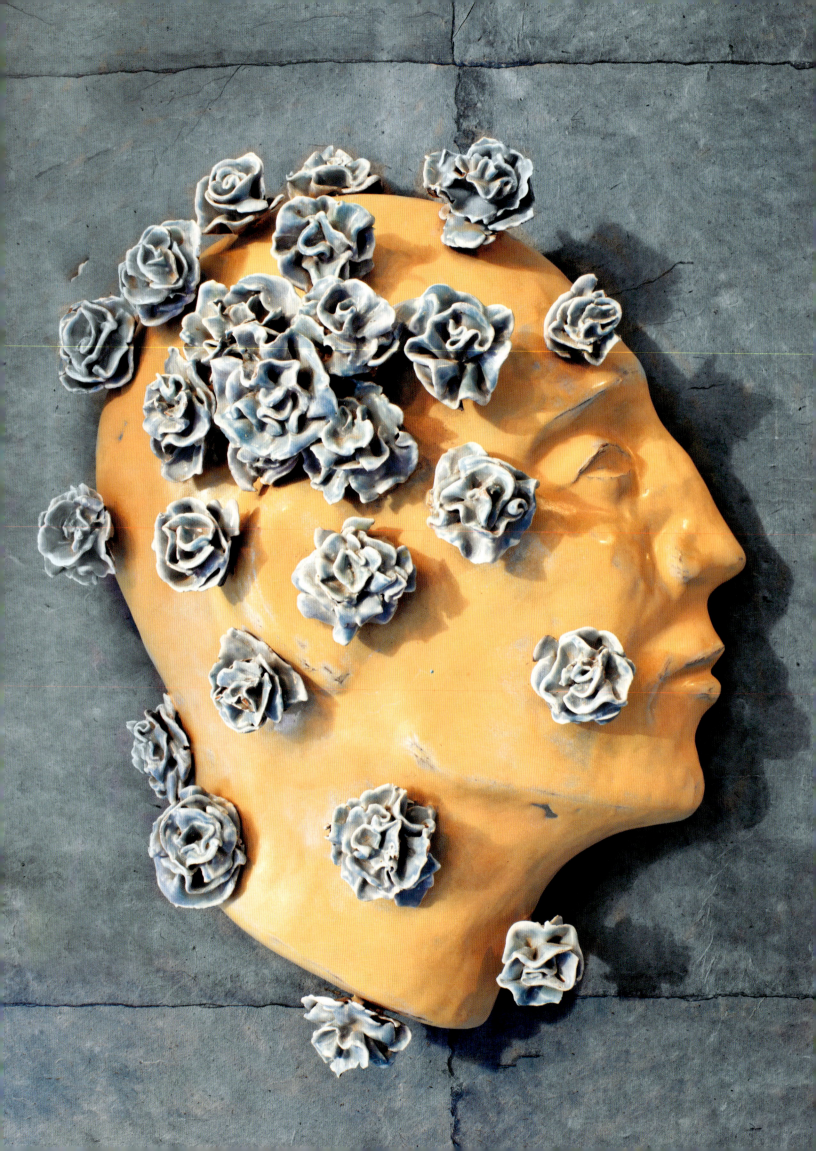

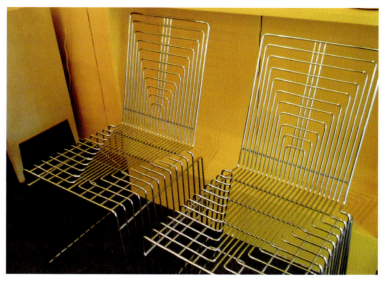

WHETHER I'M CREATING A CUSTOM PIECE AT MY METAL FABRICATOR'S STUDIO OR AM SHOPPING FOR FURNITURE WITH METAL ELEMENTS, I ALWAYS APPROACH THIS MATERIAL AS IF IT'S THE JEWELRY TO THE ROOM.

THE AZURE-BLUE OCEANO AND QUARTZITE WALL, AND THE HONED NEGRO MARQUINA MARBLE ON THE COUNTER AND BASE OF THIS CUSTOM VANITY HIGHLIGHT AND CONTRAST WITH THE WARMTH OF ITS REFLECTIVE BRONZE SINK AND LEGS.

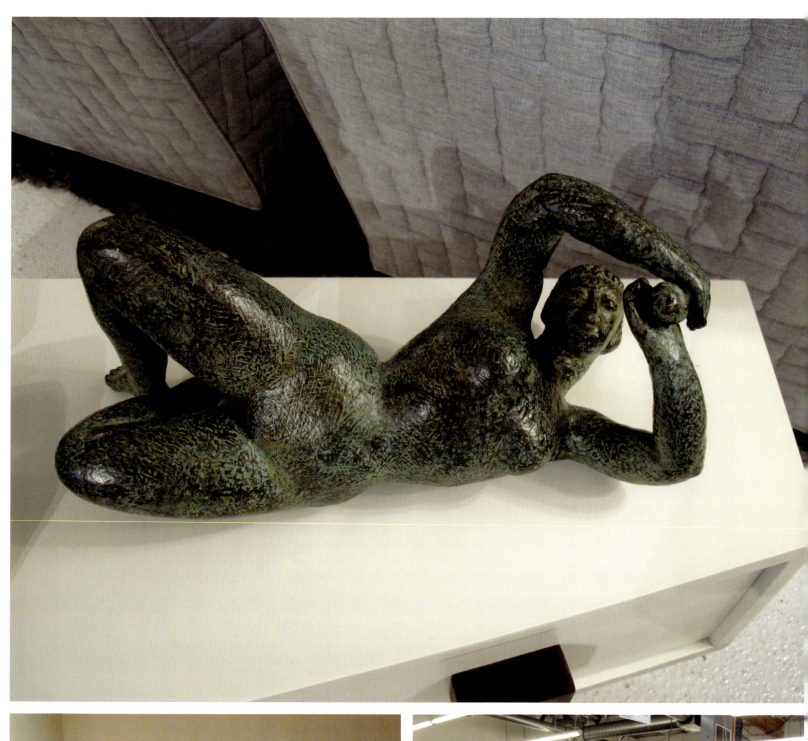

A SOFA TREATED TO LOOK LIKE PATINAED COPPER, A BRONZE SCULPTURE, OR A SMALL DETAIL ON A CHAIR... WHEREVER IT APPEARS, METAL BRINGS WITH IT A SENSE OF HISTORY. IT CARRIES A WEIGHTINESS THAT IS COMFORTING, EARTHY, AND RICH.

DON'T BE AFRAID TO MIX METALS. DOING SO GIVES A RICHNESS TO A SPACE AND SERVES TO BEAUTIFULLY HIGHLIGHT VARIOUS ELEMENTS, LIKE THIS CHAIR FRAMED IN A POLISHED NICKEL ALONGSIDE THE LAMP IN GUNMETAL WITH BRASS ACCENTS AND THE ACCOMPANYING PAINTING FRAMED IN A SILVER LEAF.

I LOVE TO CREATE A METALLIC SYMPHONY BY
USING A VARIETY OF METALS THAT PLAY OFF
ONE ANOTHER. ROSE, BRONZE, AND ANTIQUE GOLD;
STAINLESS STEEL, ZINC, AND VERDIGRIS COPPER.
THESE CAN MAKE A ROOM SHINE AND BRING OUT
THE INTENSITY OF A COLOR, AS IT DOES HERE
WITH THIS SOOTHING, TURQUOISE PALETTE.

CHROMA CONSTRUCTION

IF THERE IS ONE THING I KNOW, IT IS THAT THE COLOR OF A ROOM HAS A PROFOUND IMPACT ON THE MOOD AND ENERGY OF ITS INHABITANTS.

But that doesn't mean that I tread lightly with color. Quite the contrary, as with the great works of art, whether paintings or poetry, there is genius in boldness. Fortunately, in this case, it is not a genius that is out of reach. All it requires is a willingness to make mistakes and to experiment, with a few considerations for the laws of attraction.

Before I put brush to wall, I take careful stock of the room vistas. What do you see when you look outside the window? Is there a massive, brown oak tree, or a patinaed bronze chimney turned green by years of exposure to the elements? Perhaps a terra-cotta brick wall dominates the landscape, as was the case with a master bedroom that I filled with complementary shades of gray, blue, and violet. It is important too, to consider the quality of light in a space. Is it filled with direct sunlight for part of the day, or primarily lit by artificial sources? Dark colors can work beautifully in small, dark rooms, making them feel at once sexy and exclusive. Then I look up. A ceiling painted in a swath of bold color will add a brilliant new perspective to even an architecturally simple room. Moldings too offer an opportunity to experiment with color. Imagine a black lacquered room with the most beautiful magenta trim.

Contrary to the impression they give, monochromatic environments can also require a good measure of creativity. A guest bedroom at first glance appears entirely colored in creamy white, but upon closer inspection you will discover it has no fewer than four different shades of the clean, open tint. The linen upholstery on the bed frame is colored Plaster of Paris, the walls are Cotton Ball, the window coverings are Ecru, and the bedding is whitest of all in Ocean Pearl. Then, like a stroke of eyeliner across a beautiful, nude eye, a few sharply contrasting elements can add drama and anchor the space. Dark Mica window jambs accomplished this feat beautifully in this warm, white environment.

Wherever the spirit moves you, follow it. Toss aside convention, eschew the derivative, and never be afraid of bold colors. Though my clients will sometimes fear the intensity of a bold choice, they often discover that through that boldness emerges the calmest, most favored room in their home.

AN IMPRESSIVE PIECE OF POLYCHROMATIC
ART IS MADE MORE SO WHEN ACCOMPANIED
BY TWO IMPORTANT ARCHITECTURAL CHAIRS

THIS ROOM WAS GIVEN VOICE BY A CONTEMPORARY
PAINTING RICHLY POPULATED WITH PERIWINKLES,
GINGER PINKS, VIOLETS, MAGENTAS, SCARLET REDS,
AND DOVE GRAYS. I LATER FOUND A BEAUTIFUL
VINTAGE SET OF MARBLED CHINA AND COMBINED
IT WITH GRAPHIC CONTEMPORARY DINNERWARE,
BOTH OF WHICH COMPLEMENT THE ART BEHIND
IT AND THE ROOM AROUND THEM.

COLOR MAKES A ROOM COMPLETE. THOUGH I AM OFTEN VERY DELIBERATE WITH MY COLOR COMPOSITIONS, SOMETIMES IT CAN HAPPEN RANDOMLY WHEN I SEE DIFFERENT-HUED FABRICS INTERACTING ON A TRAY. THIS SPARK OF INSPIRATION WILL OFTEN COME TO LIFE THROUGH THE CREATION OF CUSTOM PAINT COLORS. I LOVE TO EXPERIMENT AND SO CONCEIVE FRESH CHROMATIC STORIES FOR EVERY PROJECT.

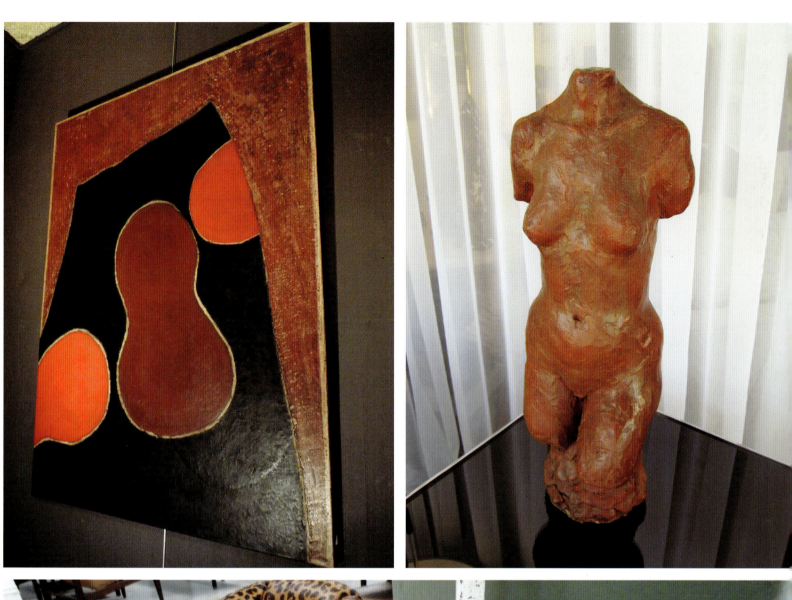

COLOR IS ESSENTIAL. IT'S THE SPIRIT OF A ROOM, THE HEART AND SOUL OF A PAINTING. IT DEFINES SHAPE. IT JUSTIFIES EVERYTHING.

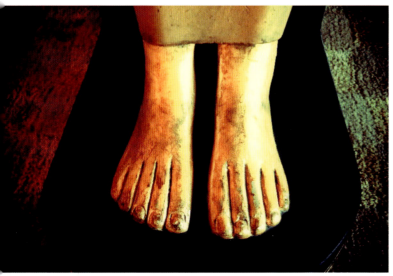

BE OPEN TO UNUSUAL COLOR COMBINATIONS AND TO STRONG, CONFIDENT HUES. NEVER ALLOW RULES ABOUT COLOR USAGE TO RESTRICT YOUR SELF-EXPRESSION.

THE BRIGHT QUALITY OF THESE NEOCLASSICAL
GOLD-LEAF ITALIAN CHAIRS DRAWS OUT THE
DEEP SCARLET RED OF THE MODERN
ART PIECE.

THE CONVERSATION PIECE IN THIS ROOM
IS THIS PICASSO-ESQUE MULTICOLORED
JEWEL OF A SCULPTURE. IT ADDS A LITTLE
SPARKLE IN THE MONOCHROMATIC
CINNABAR ENVIRONMENT.

CURATED COMPOSITIONS

10 – 11
Vintage Paul Evans dining room chairs upholstered with splatter metallic leather hide.

12 – 13
Impactful large-scale sculpture underneath a vintage glass chandelier.

Marble console supported by a pair of powerful bronze 1970s figures.

14 – 15
Studded, dimensional faux-bois paneling in a family room.

16 – 17
Scarlet red-lacquered 1970s French goatskin desk with brass detail.

18 – 19
A tray filled with bejewelment.

20 – 21
Still life with an Italian vintage typewriter.

22 – 23
An art wall of mixed media in this loft dining room.

24 – 25
Dining table comprised of three perforated brass tables.

26 – 27

1960s vintage decoupage screen

28 – 29
Elevated seating area in a New York City loft with skyline views.

30 – 31
Graphic, organic cerused ash wood floor and wall paneling.

32 – 33
Snapshots from a shopping trip in London.

34 – 35
Dramatic 1940s French sculpture in plaster of Paris in front of a contemporary piece of art.

Hand-painted wall covering in a raw ivory silk in an acoustic family room.

36 – 37
Organic, hand-painted wall covering paired with graphic ivory-and-ebony walnut floors.

1980s vintage faux-marble console paired with a 1970s cinnabar snake mirror.

38 – 39
1960s Italian side chair in black patent leather.

40 – 41
Pair of refined custom-made twin beds ruched in delicate leather.

Guest bedroom with ivory-and-ebony diagonally striped walnut floors and red alligator Kelly Wearstler chair.

42 – 43
Guest bathroom installed in an op art manner using Calcutta gold and Bardiglio marble with a lacquered goatskin vanity.

44 – 45
Deco-inspired entry vestibule with many doors and openings organized by repetitive mirrored panels.

46 – 47
Fuschia alligator chairs are the focal point in this dramatic office.

48 – 49

Beautifully composed wall of art and sculpture.

Ombre-patterned, hand-painted wall covering unifies a multifaceted ceiling.

50 – 51
Snapshots from a shopping trip to New York and Paris.

52 – 53
Still life of art and objects of art.

Punk-inspired girl's bathroom.

54 – 55
Green apple branches against a hand-painted canvas.

FETISH OF FORM

58 – 59
Bird's-eye view of a sweeping grand staircase.

Undulating, handmade white leather hand railing.

60 – 61
Intense marble combinations and a torso sculpture in a stately man's bathroom.

62 – 63
Refined turn-of-the-century classical sculpture against a hand-painted raw wall covering.

64 — 65

Optical walnut parquet floor in a dramatic kitchen.

Surrealist art on a kitchen wall.

66 — 67
Still life of four graphic Kelly Wearstler dinnerware settings.

68 — 69
Reflective bronze coffee table expands an intimate family room.

Bronze custom-made étagère showcases a client's china.

70 — 71
Moments from a shopping trip in New York.

72 — 73
Master bedroom with custom bronze and ruched leather bedframe inspired by a fireplace screen.

Hammered bronze and lacquered walnut cabinet.

74 — 75
18th-century torso.

Turn-of-the-century classical goddess sculpture.

76 — 77
Still life of the morning after.

78 — 79
Moving 1970s French decorative metal wall sculpture in a glamorous stairwell.

80 — 81
Triumvirate of wood-paneled pantry doors in an inviting kitchen.

82 — 83
Inspiration tray of adornments.

84 — 85
Dimensional wood paneling finished with bronze details in a man's closet.

Multi-drawer, lacquered goatskin vanity adorned with bronze hardware and detailing.

86 — 87
Book-matched onyx coexists with a variety of graphic marbles in this serenely timeless lady's grand bathroom.

88 — 89

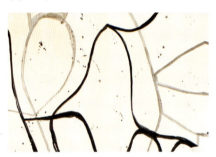

Artful hand-painted wall covering in a guest bedroom.

90 — 91
A fearless placement of art on art.

92 — 93
Graded antique mirror and marble on the walls of a fluid pool pavilion bathroom.

94 — 95
Repetitive walnut faux-bois painted cabinet with bronze detail in an architecturally challenging, multifunctioning office/closet.

96 — 97
Shopping for objects and architectural elements in Los Angeles, Italy, and New York.

98 — 99
Roman bronze god stands in an entry vestibule.

1970s French commode curated with artifacts and objects of art.

100 — 101
Daring geometric collision in a closet entry.

RAW AND REFINED

104 — 105
Mezzanine view of a 1970s vintage modern beach house.

106 — 107
Pair of bronze fanciful birds placed against a Stan Bitters custom fireplace.

108 — 109
Sculptural still life in front of a piece of vintage mixed-media art.

110 — 111

Custom wall covering mimics petrified wood in a guest bedroom.

112 — 113
Still life in women's dressing closet.

Mirror-faced cabinet doors conceal an incredibly detailed drawer setting in this highly organized woman's closet.

114 — 115
A sculptural open staircase unifies the many floors of this home.

Dominant vintage tapestry in a reading nook.

116 – 117
Inspired cedar wood master bath.

118 – 119
Commanding resin-fractured dining table.

120 – 121
Raw and refined details in an inspiration tray.

122 – 123
Loft space with harmonious through line.

124 – 125
Round French snake antique mirror reflects the room beyond.

Vertically placed mixed-media wall art is juxtaposed with a striped custom credenza.

126 – 127
Rhythmic lighting and mirrored doors expand a narrow hallway.

Carefully curated worldly objects in a master bedroom suite entry.

128 – 129
Shopping for sculpture in Italy and New York.

130 – 131

Detail of luminous Stan Bitters art.

Terrace with artful Stan Bitters wall fountain.

132 – 133
Bulbous, silk-covered sofa in the sitting area of a guest bedroom.

Leather ruched bed inspired by the organic form of a shell in a beachside vintage home.

134 – 135
Bronze bedside chests are the jewelry in a master bedroom.

136 – 137
Greek-key shower doors against a raw organic marble in an impactful bathroom.

Marble skinned bathroom with vanity and vintage music chair.

138 – 139
Art deco-inspired silk carpet and espresso-brown 1960s Italian leather chairs.

140 – 141
Fine vintage metal Warren Platner chairs in an intimate dining room.

Delicate herringbone-patterned floors and slated window grills in an energetic kitchen.

142 – 143

1940s French chairs upholstered in tie-dyed suede in a reading room.

144 – 145
Newly commissioned Sheila Hicks wall tapestry grounds a tranquil sitting room.

146 – 147
Shopping trip to Paris, New York, and Los Angeles.

148 – 149
Exposed-grain wooden chair in a room with textured marble walls and floors.

Antique burl-wood seating alongside marble walls and floors in a beachside resort lobby.

150 – 151
Alpaca vintage Italian chair and patinaed copper cabinet.

152 – 153
Lovely ceramic bosom vase, the focal point in a still life.

154 – 155
Engaging conversation between wall art and sculpture in a salon.

METALLIFEROUS

158 – 159

Hand-applied silver gold-leaf panels with bronze details and beautifully articulated squares and rectangles in a jewel box of a closet.

160 – 161
Twenty-two-foot negro marquina marble fireplace in a dramatic two-story library.

Unlacquered custom bronze circular staircase with perforated stair risers.

162 – 163
Staircase railing in an unlacquered bronze.

164 – 165
Marble wall in the kitchen of a New York City loft.

Gunmetal front door studded with copper pyramids.

166 – 167
In this music room, an interesting composition of chairs creates a beautiful melody.

168 — 169
1940s Italian plaque as art.

Bar with skyline views in a New York City pied-à-terre.

170 — 171
Sparkling bar still life.

172 — 173
Bronze bar étagère is the jewelry in this indulgent kitchen.

Traveling bar set up for an evening of mixing.

174 — 175
A shopping trip to London, San Francisco, and Paris; creating product in my studio; and a few snake clutches from a vintage show in Los Angeles.

176 — 177
Stonework, at once exhilarating and tranquil in a powder room.

178 — 179

Op art is the focal point in this boy's bedroom.

Sleek and soulful boy's bathroom, a visual playground.

180 — 181
Entry vestibule with a spirit of modern and medieval.

Decorative dormers meet 1960s Italian playfulness in this child's bedroom.

182 — 183
Dramatic chevron-patterned walnut floors in a stylish, chic pool pavilion.

184 — 185
Velvet malachite-inspired sofa, marble coffee table, and dynamic art in a penthouse terrace-adjacent media room.

Evocative green parchment-tiled wall covering.

186 — 187
Striped bedside chests engage with counter-striped rug in a boy's bedroom.

Parisian bust used as a canvas.

188 — 189
A shopping trip to a stone yard in Italy; a visit to a leather company; shopping in San Francisco.

190 — 191
Cool composition of art, furniture, and lighting.

192 — 193
Jubilee of color, pattern, art, and Legos in a child's playroom.

Happy still life of artwork and beautiful pastels.

194 — 195
A turquoise tray housing objects of desire.

196 — 197
Bird's-eye view into a beautifully spirited library.

Pretty composition comprised of many different hands of plaster, bronze, canvas, mirror, and wood.

198 — 199
Bold hand-painted silk wall covering is the backdrop for graphic objects of art.

Edgy and refined private receiving room.

CHROMA CONSTRUCTION

202 — 203
Elegant violet-saturated dining room with raw solid-oak table.

204 — 205

Custom cubist-inspired wool carpet in a living room.

1950s California bronze wall medallion against a hand-troweled wall covering.

206 — 207
Pair of important French industrial chairs stand guard in front of a complicated oil painting.

208 — 209
Soaring bronze Italian sconces add height and drama to this living room of pairs.

210 — 211
Gold flatware and contemporary violet dinnerware with gold detail sit atop a raw oak table.

Art deco cabinet against a raw wall covering and crowned by a gold-leaf ceiling.

212 — 213
1930s Russian cubist painting behind a beautiful mix of contemporary and vintage china.

214 — 215
Soulful periwinkle bar sparkles with its many metal details and citron chairs.

216 — 217

Composition with a rare blue bird, Picasso-esque vase, and Roman master head on its side on a back bar.

218 — 219

Cinnabar tray with color swatches, rug samples, and marble elements.

220 — 221

Monumental geometric obelisque sculpture next to a modern oil painting and a baroque chair in an unexpected leather.

Beautifully aged antique mirror atop a marble fireplace with egg mise-en scéne reflects 1940s Murano glass chandelier in the room beyond.

222 — 223

Explosive hand-forged metal starburst sculpture.

Luxe rosy-hued powder room creates a flattering environment.

224 — 225

A colorful shopping trip to Greece, Paris, and London.

226 — 227

Pair of massive cerulean blue leather sofas rests atop a rhythmic carpet and in front of rhythmic wall paneling in a media room.

228 — 229

Visually stimulating monochromatic still life.

Striking color on this Ettore Sottsass-inspired cabinet.

230 — 231

Floral explosion in an array of decorative vessels.

232 — 233

Thematic play on color in a sexy master bedroom.

Lacquered desk and cabinets create a dramatic height in this room.

234 — 235

Organic raw canvas juxtaposed with linear desk and cabinets.

236 — 237

Shopping trip to an art gallery in Paris; a favorite leather shop in New York; and moments from the Los Angeles studio.

238 — 239

Still life with bronze, leather, stone, and crystal elements atop a water-snake cabinet.

240 — 241

Calming neoclassical gold chairs next to chaotic modern art.

242 — 243

Pumpkin-hued silk slubby wall covering with painted wood onyx moldings.

244 — 245

A face of wonder.

246 — 247

Twelve-foot curved sofa anchors a monochromatic room.

APPLAUSE

Every project brings with it the opportunity to collaborate with a cast of artisans, craftsmen, and talented peeps, as well as my dedicated and hardworking office team, all of whom I count among my family. They make the process fun and provide unending opportunities for enlightened experiences.

Erika Albies; Ary Anderson; Gilad Ben-Artzi; Jessica Ayromloo; Barbara Barran; Leslie Barrett; Leana Bartlett; Robina Benson; Bergdorf Goodman; Blackman Cruz; Brian Biglin; Stan Bitters; Pete Black; Oliver Bowien at Slyvan; John Bowman; Fernando Bracer; Lunch Brent; Harold Briones; Claude Brunkow; Lynda Carroll; Cristina Buckley; Richard Bullock; Brad Butler; Tim Buggs; Espy Campos; Richard Cannon; Hector Cervantes; Shelly Chaney; Bridgette Cochran; Amanda Codding; Joel Chen; Beth Coller; Michel Contessa; Nancy Corzine; Grey Crawford; Robert Crowder; Ron Dier; Adam Dorfman; Patrick Dragonette; Ana Consuelo Duarte; Eccola; Stephen Elrod; Jose Escobar; Irma Estrada; Express Electric; Mike Fair; Fat Chance; Nazy Ferdows; Darren Franks; Joseph Free; Samantha Jones at Libra Leather, Amanda Luttrell Garrigus; Lana Gomez; Francois Halard; Josh Herman; Sheila Hicks; Meredith Hill; Kimberly Holt; Paul Hooker at Sferra; I Grace Construction; Rebekah Jacobson; Mimi Jakobson; Kevin Johnson; Snow Kahn; David Kobae; Ravi Lalwani; Kwila Lee; Rocky Lefleur; Alanna Lichtwardt; Miyoko Love; Karyn Lovegrove; Guillermo Maranon; Paul Marra; Robert Masello; David McCauley; Jean de Merry; Charles Miers; Andrew Pickard Morgan at Pickard; Lauren Myers; Ellen Nidy; Eric Nyarko; Alan Olick; Pacific Hide & Leather; Raul Padilla; Luis Palacios; Kelly Porter; Amanda Price; Joel Quinones; Jose Ramirez; Carlos Rittner; Tom Robbinson; Jennifer Salinas; Jaime Sanchez; Scalamandre; Steve Sellery; David Serrano; Suzanne and Christopher Sharp at The Rug Company; Annie Schlechter; Ben Soleimani; Jerry Solomon; Aaron Stewart; Jacob Stusser; David Sutherland; Paul Sweeney; Kuang-Wei Tan; Cheryl Tarnofsky; Brian Tichenor at Tichenor & Thorp Architects Inc.; Ken Todd; Ian Tyson; Christina Watkinson; West Coast Trimmings; Lou Verhoeven; Chris Viggiano; Michael Ward; Amy Baker Williams; Wendi Williams; Robert Wilson; Rick Wooldridge.

My clients become my teachers too, through their expressed likes and dislikes and their individual creative spirits. Each bring to the work a resonance and renaissance without which I would be less successful, it is certain. To each of them I express my deeply felt gratitude.

C.D.; Heather McDowell Levin and Adam Levin; Stan, Miriam, Gabriella, and Andreas Rothbart; Jeff and Lara Sanderson; Whitney Casey and Nav Sooch.

And to my family, from whom my greatest inspiration flows, I am ever and always thankful for their boundless love and support, and their seemingly limitless enthusiasm for my creative work. Brad, Oliver and Elliott Korzen; Wayne, Nancy, and Tami Talley; Erwin and Carolyn Korzen; Kim and Greg, Matthew, Amanda, and Emma Neistat; Brooke Korzen and Derek Spalding

First published in the United States of America in 2012
by Rizzoli International Publications, Inc.
300 Park Avenue South, New York, NY 10010
www.rizzoliusa.com

All rights reserved. No parts of this publication may be reproduced,
stored in a retrieval system, or transmitted in any form or by any means,
electronic, mechanical, photocopying, recording or otherwise,
without prior approval of the publishers.

© 2012 Rizzoli International Publications, Inc.
© 2012 Kelly Wearstler, Inc.

Writer: Amanda Luttrell Garrigus
Photographers: Grey Crawford; Francois Halard; Annie Schlechter
Book Design: Amy Baker Williams with Snow Kahn

2012 2013 2014 2015 2016 / 10 9 8 7 6 5 4 3 2 1
ISBN-13: 978-0-8478-3858-5
Library of Congress Control Number: 2012941219
Printed and bound in China
Distributed to the U.S. trade by Random House

THE NEW ANTIQUARIANS

THE NEW ANTIQUARIANS

WRITTEN & CURATED BY

Michael Diaz-Griffith

PRIMARY PHOTOGRAPHY BY
BRIAN W. FERRY

MMXXIII

M

INTRODUCTION—8
The Persistent Richness of Things

CHAPTER I—14
Emily Adams Bode Aujla & Aaron Singh Aujla

CHAPTER II—32
Adam Charlap Hyman

CHAPTER III—50
Pablo Bronstein

CHAPTER IV—68
Alex Tieghi-Walker

CHAPTER V—84
Jeremy Simien

CHAPTER VI—98
Giancarlo Valle & Jane Keltner de Valle

CHAPTER VII—108
Jared Frank

CHAPTER VIII—122
Camille Okhio

CHAPTER IX—132
Collier Calandruccio

CHAPTER X—146

Kyle Marshall

CHAPTER XI—160

Sean McNanney & Sinan Tuncay

CHAPTER XII—176

Abel Sloane & Ruby Woodhouse

CHAPTER XIII—190

Emily Eerdmans

CHAPTER XIV—204

Jared Austin

CHAPTER XV—220

Avril Nolan & Quy Nguyen

CHAPTER XVI—234

Samuel Snider

CHAPTER XVII—248

Andrew LaMar Hopkins

ACKNOWLEDGMENTS—268

TO THE AFFECTIONATE MEMORY OF
PHILIP HEWAT-JABOOR

in gratitude for his encouragement of
"grown-up" collectors of all ages

Introduction

The Persistent Richness of Things

If a story begins with finding, it must end with searching.

– Penelope Fitzgerald, *The Blue Flower*

Three of anything makes a collection, but a collecting practice can be ignited, quietly, by a single bewitching object. This book honors that inaugural object and the nascent collector's first step, taken perhaps unknowingly, into a lifetime of desiring, studying, searching, and only occasionally, when the conditions are just right, finding.

A great number of young people are taking that first step today, and the images and stories in these pages demonstrate that young collectors do indeed, despite fears to the contrary, exist. I call them the New Antiquarians, not because they uniformly collect antiques—some collect vintage material, or a mix of antique, vintage, and contemporary art and objects—but because they follow, with considerable spirit and rigor, in the long, eccentric tradition of treating the practice of connoisseurship as a serious vocation. Some of the New Antiquarians are connoisseurs already, while others have progressed well down the path to becoming such. All are passionate about objects and their histories, and they have convinced me, over the past decade, that the future of historic art, antiques, and the material culture of the past is in good hands.

Why should it be otherwise, you might ask? Like romance, the collecting bug takes hold of us before we know to doubt it, and any student of history will conclude that human beings will always be, according to their nature, acquisitive. Still, in recent years, those in the know—

antiques dealers, curators, seasoned collectors—have prophesied an extinction event for collecting. To understand why, we must cast our glance back to the closing decades of the twentieth century.

Between the 1970s and early 2000s, the market for antiques and historic art ascended to precipitous heights, adding untold value to the world's store of old things. Entire categories of objects that had been considered unfashionable or even objectionable, from English furniture to American folk art, returned to vogue, along with the practice of collecting itself. Volumes could be dedicated to the economic and cultural reasons for this boom, and undoubtedly some would strike a negative tone. The period, especially the 1980s, has been characterized as an Age of Excess. For collectors and connoisseurs, however, it was a Golden Age. Objects were not just desired; they were violently contested and victoriously won, from the sharp-elbowed aisles of antiques shows to the increasingly glamorous auction house floor, which became a locus for public spectacle. There was little doubt that things mattered, and no question at all that stewards would volunteer themselves, perhaps too readily, to usher them into the next century—paying millions of dollars, if necessary, for the privilege of doing so.

The problem with booms is that they are pregnant with busts. So it was with this boom, which slid into a downturn around the turn of the century before busting, with barely a whimper, after the financial crisis of 2007–2008.

What happened? Did the recession cause collectors to tighten their belts in the usual fashion, or did the trouble go, mysteriously, deeper? Some gestured to the specter of 9/11 and the endless wars that followed, murmuring about a generational shift from beauty to survival. Others pointed to the burgeoning taste for minimalism among Gen X, or those born between roughly 1965 and 1980, which produced a mania for midcentury modern at a time when the material was still too new, despite its vintage status, to be seen through the lens of continuity rather than disruption. Meanwhile, at the bottom of the market, IKEA rose to a status first of ubiquity, then of hegemony, becoming a kind of shorthand for everything antiques lovers hated: flatness, convenience, and above all, disposability.

Historians of these times will marvel at our obliviousness to the internet's rise, even as it remade our world. While the antiques market cratered, the vast jungle gym of high society began to fail, too, reducing the stakes of socially competitive activities such as collecting, decorating, and dressing. To some it seemed the whole art of living was under attack, and certainly it was in abeyance. After three hundred years of decreasing formality, Western households embraced casual lifestyles and open floor plans, foregoing dinner parties in favor of gatherings around the kitchen island or aggressively disaggregated happenings around the house. AOL Instant Messenger did not require the use of hats, gloves, and stoles. It barely required the use of a chair.

At the height of the antiques boom, by contrast, an ambitious couple on the Upper East Side could be expected to own a set of eighteenth-century dining chairs in the manner of Thomas Chippendale or John Linnell. Their counterparts in Kansas City might have acquired clever reproductions of relatively recent manufacture—not because they could not afford originals, but because there simply were not enough to go around. In Alabama, where I was born and raised, overpriced nineteenth-century imitations or "cheap and nasty" modern reproductions (to borrow a phrase from William Morris) would have exuberantly filled the same gap.

Thirty years later, however, few cared if you had a dining room or not, and the chairs gathered around your table (if you had one) were immaterial to your social existence (if you had one). In a digital age of ultimate plurality, one style was as good as another. If you collected, with few exceptions, it was for love of the thing itself.

Against this backdrop, the grande dame of the antiques world, New York City's Winter Antiques Show, soldiered on. When I joined the fair in 2015, eager to help dust it off, I found that the pinnacle of the antiques market had stubbornly refused to collapse, or its collapse was slow enough to evade detection by the naked eye. Sometimes, late at night, I suspected the latter. Serious Discussions were convened, and over glossy conference tables and glasses of Champagne it was agreed that masterworks would always be in demand; institutions and the very rich would continue paying good money, as they are designed to do, for the best. But what of everyday collectors—the kind who might buy a set of chairs for their dining room? Would there appear a new wave of moderately wealthy, eccentric, or foolhardy enthusiasts ready to offer themselves up at the altar of collecting? Sometimes my colleagues looked to me, the lone twentysomething in the room, to answer this question. Sometimes they did not.

I found both responses to my presence highly motivating.

As I walked around the fair's event for younger people, begun in the nineties by the children of board members, I ran a sort of diagnostic test through gimlet eyes. I had attended Young Collectors Night before, but as a guest pursuing my lifelong hunt for art and objects of fascination. Now, on a different mission, I surveyed a troubling scene: cash-fattened bankers accompanied by mysterious beauties in red dresses; stands abandoned by their exhibitors and, like crime scenes, cordoned off from visitors; and a provisional DJ booth, vibrating with tinny sound, that doubled as a drop-off for drained drinks.

Dealers referred to the proceedings as "The Young and the Checkless," and I understood why. No one was buying. Of even greater concern: few were looking. The Upper East Siders who cochaired the event huddled together, making the most of their unwieldy creation, and on paper their party was a success: it raised desperately needed funds for the show's charity beneficiary, East Side House Settlement, a community-based organization in the South Bronx. It did not reflect a new wave of interest in anything, however, much less historic art and antiques. Quite the opposite. Here was the bust on display for all comers to see—or anyone with $200 and a Thursday evening to spare.

The good thing about busts is that they are pregnant with booms, and happily I sensed a boom brewing in other quarters. Millennials had begun retaining, rather than dispossessing, inherited heirlooms, and dredging affordable treasures from overlooked reefs of unwanted objects. Nostalgia was in the air. On the still-novel digital app Instagram, people of all ages discovered a dematerialized temple of beauty, posting—and feverishly discussing—obscure historic interiors, works of art unearthed in newly digitized museum archives, old photographs of vintage fashion, and objects of every description. On Tumblr, the youngest people alive—the world's first "digital natives"—assembled collections of history-related ephemera, some of it ironizing (on-set shots of Kirsten Dunst, in costume as Marie Antoinette, taking a smoke break) and some of it earnest, even academic in scope. At Gucci, the Italian fashion house known for its sleek, nocturnal brand of glamour, creative director Alessandro Michele was beginning to engineer one of the great turnarounds in fashion history, devising a complex new set of codes for the house derived, with an impish gusto that grew each season, from historical references. It came as no surprise that his Instagram account enjoyed cult status; it was, like an increasing number of others, a panoply of gently decaying palazzi and idiosyncratic personal collections. For even more palazzo porn, lovers of beauty could subscribe to *Cabana*, a biannual bible of soulful interiors layered, invariably, with collections. Later, as Michele's star waned at Gucci, other collector-designers rose in the firmament: Jonathan Anderson, creative director of Spanish fashion house Loewe, featured a king's ransom of Rococo candlesticks from the mid-1750s in an advertising campaign that went viral among Very Online antiquarians.

Meanwhile, at the monthly shelter magazines, editors once again commissioned stories featuring ruffle-and-bow-bedecked interiors. At fashion presentations on the Lower East Side and London, young brands—Batsheva, Bode, Palomo Spain, Puppets and Puppets—embraced historical references, too, and those presentations soon became Fashion Week–sanctioned runway shows. In the arts and pop culture, figuration and gestures toward the Old Masters proliferated, from the work of artists such as Kehinde Wiley and Salman Toor to Beyoncé and Jay-Z's "Apeshit" music video, which was part homage, part institutional critique of the art-historical complex. A spirit of retro-postmodern play moved through the realm of collectible design, then the culture at large, followed by a kooky wave of neosurrealism and the arrival of "medieval modern," a Gen Z–meets–Axel Vervoordt expression of historicist minimalism. Everywhere, it seemed, everyone spoke of craft—that is, the old ways of making things by hand. With mounting excitement, I cofounded a connoisseurship-focused affinity group for young collectors in 2018, the New Antiquarians, and documented the vibe shift on my Instagram account. Where else?

None of this resulted in a sudden change of fortune for the world's store of old things. Antiques and historic art were returning to favor as references, but collecting has never been a young person's game, and for good reason: it requires disposable income. Free-spenders and the childless enjoy a head start, with young parents and the financially prudent following behind as money allows. As we freshened up the Winter Show and turned around Young Collectors Night, and as I began working with galleries, auction houses, museums, magazines, and other fairs, helping them stoke—and prepare for—this burgeoning wave of interest, a cynic would occasionally challenge me: "Where," gesturing around, "are the new clients?" A dealer once insisted he would not engage with younger people until they proved themselves worthwhile by beginning to buy, making the first move in the courtship dance that is the dealer-client relationship. He wanted, he said, to be wise. I understood his reticence. Quite possibly he owned a warehouse of unsold material from the time before the bust. But wisdom has its limits. One day soon the pendulum would swing, bust would become boom, and we would wake up in a new world.

We live in that new world today. Young collectors do indeed, despite fears to the contrary, exist, and this book is evidence of their existence. At antiques shows and auctions, these New Antiquarians not only look, but buy. Online and in these pages, they share their collections—considered, here, in the context of their homes. They do not collect due to social pressure; they collect for love of the thing itself. While some hail from families with a collecting gene, others, including myself, began collecting ex nihilo. In a digital age of ultimate plurality, we are choosing the material culture of the past, or it is choosing us. For collectors of color, queer collectors, and first-generation collectors, that choice—or calling—can be freighted with complexity, but it is also charged with possibility. Collecting is a tradition, but an eccentric one, and it is carried out most capably by freethinkers who prize self-expression, the pursuit of an individual sensibility, and the discovery—often through old things—of the new.

As you will see in the pages to follow, the New Antiquarians do the new as well as the antique. Some mix or display objects in new-fashioned ways, while others reclaim or recontextualize history through the things they have chosen to steward and interpret. A few, brilliantly, do all of these things at once. In their collections and stories, it is my hope that you will find surprise, delight, and inspiration for your own collecting practice.

Finding, after all, is only the beginning of the story. Once you've been bewitched, the search begins again—for more objects, for their true nature, and for your own, poised restlessly between the future and the past.

Mexico City
December 1, 2022

I

EMILY ADAMS BODE AUJLA & AARON SINGH AUJLA

Chinatown, New York City

Handmade dollhouse furniture, American quilts and linsey-woolsey coverlets, Alsace pottery, Bengali literature, senior corduroys, and vintage Chanel.

Among collectors, there are those who collect objects as objects, fixated on the particularity—the thinginess—of each thing they acquire. These objects could land in a private gallery, a hoarder's heap, a storage facility, or any other place where a thing can be visited and beheld, cradled, and considered. At the end of each visit the door can be shut, the box can be closed, and the object can be trusted to retreat, unseen, into its auratic singularity.

Then there are world-building collectors like Emily Adams Bode Aujla and Aaron Singh Aujla, for whom objects are the material of life, not discrete things to be collected in isolation. In the designers' Chinatown loft, each object tells a story, reflects a craft tradition, reveals a personal reference, or participates in a ritual of everyday life, and most—as far as I can see—perform all of these actions at once, in dialogue with each other and their stewards, and in harmony with the purpose-built environment that houses them all.

If Emily and Aaron were not designers, the world they are building, object by object, would simply be that of their apartment: a complex, Cape Cod–meets-Chandigarh cosmos swirling above Lower Manhattan. Designers they are, however,

and prolific ones at that, and the world they are building, project by project, has no known edges.

For Emily, a preservationist to the bone, history is alive in the present, and our emotional connection to the past—down to its most mundane processes, such as mending worn textiles—imbues contemporary life with a richer meaning. It is no coincidence that the seasonal collections for her fashion brand, Bode, are autobiographical in scope. When viewed together, they amount to a vast scrapbook of memory derived from her own life, the lives of family and friends, and the lives of objects she has known. On sourcing trips, I imagine Emily neck-deep and deeply happy amid mounds of antique and vintage textiles at the Brimfield Antique Flea Market, or rummaging through dusty but perfectly preserved trousseaux in Provence: cutwork, bobbin lace, unused bedsheets, and monogrammed napkins, all ready to be documented, aired out, and circulated back into life.

In her world, a supply of deadstock fabric may be sewn up into new clothes, tailored for future memories but charged with an ineffable feeling for the past. A particularly precious textile, on the other hand, might be archived, studied, and reproduced by Bode's artisans and tailors, requiring them to learn—and thus preserve—extinct (or nearly so) craftways in the process. This is preservation in its truest sense, running through objects as well as the hands that make them.

Of course, an object might also be kept at home, accessioned to a growing collection. This is where Aaron enters the frame. Like a nineteenth-century curator, respectful of objects but particularly sensitive to their aesthetic presentation, he is responsible, as often as not, for the placement of Emily's finds. The couple's collaboration at home mirrors their work together, although detecting the hair-thin boundary between life and work, with these two, is a fool's errand. Over a decade ago, Emily influenced Aaron's shift from the fine arts to the realm of furniture design and interiors; meanwhile, Aaron and Benjamin Bloomstein, his partner in the research-based design studio Green River Project, a sort of literary-historical think tank with saws, helped conceive of Bode's immersive, narrative-driven presentations. In recent years, building on those ephemeral displays, they conjured the growing brand's numinous tobacco-stained-and-scalloped stores. Like the built environment of Bode and the apartment pictured here, Green River Project's quarterly collections begin with a set of Bauhausian parameters that are dizzyingly upended, or sharply clarified, through engagement with historical references from tramp art and natural history museums to the films of Satyajit Ray.

Old, but with a sense of futurity. New, but with a sense for the past.

For those concerned with the display of *things*, Emily and Aaron's apartment could be a model for the private gallery in our post–white cube age, drenched in mustard-yellow paint and suggestively screened as it is, yet formally clarified enough to serve as a showplace for objects. Even so, it is not a place where a thing can be visited and beheld, cradled and considered, and then put away. There is no door for shutting or lid for closing. The objects on display are immanent and everywhere, and the material of life spreads all around.